A Child's Eye View of Astrology

By Cynthia Cassandra

Look for other A Child's Eye View titles:

A Child's Eye View of Heathenry An in-depth look at the modern practice of Heathenry intended for young readers and their parents.

A Child's Eye View of Vodou Designed to make the practice of Haitian Vodou understandable and non-threatening to children and parents.

A Child's Eye View of Wicca An excellent intro to Wicca for people of all ages.

A Child's Eye View of Magick A definitive introduction to Magick for anyone curious about the Occult.

A Child's Eye View of Tarot A perfect introduction for all ages to Tarot reading.

Coming Soon:

A Child's Eye View of Fair Folk
A Child's Eye View of Divination
A Child's Eye View of Totems and Tutelary Spirits
A Child's Eye View of Chakras
And much more…

A Child's Eye View of Astrology

By Cynthia Cassandra

Interior and cover imagery by Bekki Leddon

Spero Publishing
Madison, WI

ISBN 978-1-105-27329-2

Publishing maintains a website at http://speropublishing.webs.com/.
Upcoming products, news, and book reviews may be found there.

Contact the owner through the "Contact Us" form at
http://speropublishing.webs.com/

-or-

Alan Leddon
Spero Publishing
PO Box 8747
Madison, WI

Table of Contents

Introduction

Hey, do you know what Astrology is about?

This small book is just an insight onto Astrology. It is important to know that Astrology is much more than just Zodiac signs. Actually, Zodiac signs only tell us where the Sun was when we were born; there are 9 other celestial bodies, 12 houses, and literally thousands of aspects that have to be taken into consideration when casting a chart and analyzing it.

Astrology is a perfect instrument for self-discovery and prediction based on our personality traits as described by our chart, but it requires a lot of study and practice in order to be accurate. Personally, I feel Astrology is quite different from Tarot and other divinatory arts, though astrological symbols may be used for divination and even magick (if you know them well enough). So Astrology helps us to be acquainted with all the facets of our real Self. If you are bold and if you persevere enough to unveil its mysteries, you may be rewarded endlessly with a rigorous and to-the-point explanation of your inner strengths and weaknesses. Knowing yourself is a powerful advantage, no matter the world you live in. An inscription at the entrance of the Delphic Oracle said *Know Thyself and you will know the Universe*. If you have discipline and vision to explore Astrology fully, you can reach the point of mastering yourself and thus mastering the manifestation of events and things around you. Otherwise you can also use Astrology as a powerful knowledge tool. It is your choice.

So, the real question is... how much do you want to know about Astrology?

Chapter 1

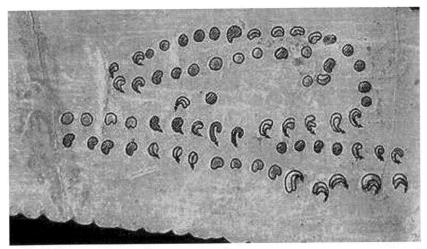

We have some evidence of astrological calculations, including lunar cycles marked on bones and cave walls, dating back as far as 35,000 years ago. However, in writing, we can trace Western Tropical Astrology back to the Sumerian king *Sargon of Akkad* (2334 – 2279 B.C.E.). From then on, many civilizations developed very complete systems of predicting some events related to mundane life and also spiritual knowledge. In Western Europe and ancient America, Astrology was present in life areas such as medicine, herbs, and decisions. It was in the Middle Ages that the predictive character of Astrology was perfected through wise men such as Nostradamus.

Meanwhile, China and India, as well as other civilizations, developed complex astrological systems. In this small book, however, we only will look at Western Tropical Astrology.

We can relate to judiciary astrology, that is to say, astrology applied to people. It is quite a recent development that the predictive power of Astrology has been focused on specific individuals. In very ancient times, the common good was more important than individual well-being, so, usually, Astrology was used to determine possible outcomes of battles, kings and queens' births, decisions that could affect the entire community, and to predict the crops' seasonal cycles. Today, we can also work with other analysis themes such as health, business, karma and human resources astrology. All of these topics belong to judiciary astrology.

Western Tropical Astrology is the system commonly used by astrologers in Europe and U.S.A. Of course, astrologers know the Universe is not static and that it is ever-changing, but they prefer to use the Zodiac as it was meant and designed in the ancient days. According this original Zodiac, the vernal equinox occurs yearly in what the astrologers say the 0° of Aries. Thus we call this method the symbolic zodiac.

There is an ongoing argument about the accuracy of Western Tropical Astrology due to the fact that actual constellations and zodiac placements are not aligned the same way they were when Astrology was born and developed in Babylon, Chaldea and Egypt. There are some astrologers working presently towards a new system based on accurate placements (check out Jade Sol Luna's website at http://www.hiddenmoon.com/) according to data used on astronomical calculations.

In Astrology (Western Tropical Astrology) we work with the four elements: Fire, Earth, Air and Water. We also take into consideration the three qualities: cardinal, fixed and mutable.

Presently we work with 10 celestial bodies: the Sun, the Moon, Mercury, Venus, Mars, Jupiter, Saturn, Uranus, Neptune and Pluto, each one being the regent and/or co-regent of one or more Zodiac signs.

The Zodiac signs are: Aries, Taurus, Gemini, Cancer, Leo, Virgo, Libra, Scorpio, Sagittarius, Capricorn, Aquarius and Pisces.

On a deeper level, there are the aspects that unite planets: conjunction, sextile, square, trine and opposition, besides other aspects that contribute to the birth chart analysis.

Chapter 2

Astrology explains reasons behind apparent unrelated events. You can actually get to know people through the movements of the planets through their birth charts. We call these movements *transits* and their influence may be more or less lasting depending the nature of the planets (they can either be *fast* such as the Sun, the Moon, Mercury, Venus and Mars or *slow* paced, such as Jupiter, Saturn, and also the slower ones such as Uranus, Neptune, and Pluto).

Why are you rich or poor? Why are you fast or slow, strong or weak, successful or not? Why do you gain so much weight when others do not? Astrology works not by magick, clairvoyance or intuition, but through a sensitive interpretation of the knowledge engraved on an astral chart.

Happiness and success are goals in everyone's lives and, to find that, many people go to a professional astrologer. Unfortunately many people tend to confuse happiness with money, a good marriage, or social status and power. A great bank account or a good marriage doesn't necessarily lead to a happy life. One of the most important aspects of life is work; Astrology can help you study better and to choose your future career.

Your individual chart will tell you, if correctly read, your dream job, the illnesses that will probably affect you, the sort of people with whom marriage can work for you, and a lot of other precious details. So explore your birth chart in order to know your strengths and weaknesses.

Chapter 3

Astrology works by casting a chart, done today through proper software and by analyzing it.

Here we will focus on analysis, because any serious free website can give you detailed information about your chart.

Analyze your chart. In Chapter IV you can find out some experiments that can give you a better knowledge of yourself, your family and friends.

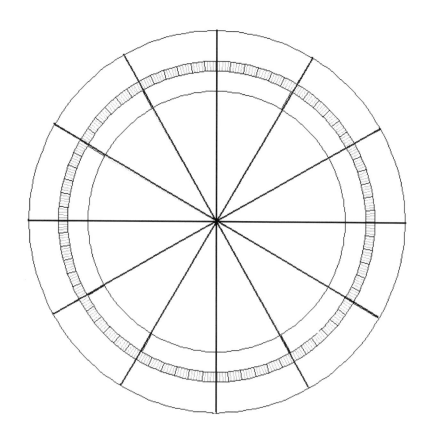

Elements

The first chart analysis you can get is through the four elements that reflect your basic energy signature. Check them out:

FIRE – Symbolizes the spirit inspiration. Action, enthusiasm, leadership and radiance are the most common traits related with this element. It is associated with creativity, vitality, intuition, optimism, transmutation, aspiration, intelligence, victories and conquests of many sorts.

EARTH – It is the manifestation realm of the spiritual. The material concerns take over, as well as discipline, method and sensual pleasures. It is associated with the physical body and the five senses, fertility, practical sense, permanence, roots, productivity, basic needs, safety, caution.

AIR – It is the intellect realm. Planning, communicating, travelling and gossip are very usual between air people. It is associated with the mind, movement, books, grace, companionship, computers, TV, ideas, mental stability, technology, concepts, introspection, innovation and planning.

WATER – It is the emotional realm. Love, friendship, past experiences, home, feelings and imagination are strong in this element. It is associated with emotions, cleanness, empathy, softness, protection, fluidity, cycles, passivity, sensitivity, reflection, compassion, imagination and illusion.

Energy type

Now, after the elements we have to consider the three qualities, meaning the way you apply your specific energy type.

CARDINAL – Leading the way and putting things in motion. This Cardinal quality implies action, entrepreneur spirit, challenge, affirmation, initiation, change, leadership and impetus.

FIXED – Maintaining the status quo and the order of things. It reflects consistency, stiffness, resistance, stability, firmness, loyalty, limits, and predictability.

MUTABLE – Ever-changing things in order to get closer and closer to perfection. It refers to flexibility, versatility, mutability, unpredictability, instability and superficiality.

Planets

Then we can check out our planets. Planets are very important for a horoscope, because the way they are placed in a sign or house shows or hides their particular power.

However, there are specific signs with which specific planets have a great affinity. It is as if you have a planet ruling a specific sign; that makes that particular planet very powerful whenever it happens to be placed in that specific sign —we call that *planetary rulerships* or *co-rulerships*. When you find this in your own chart, it means that that planet has all its strength applied to the sign and house in which is placed. The opposite of planetary rulership is the detriment, meaning the planet is placed in a sign opposed to its natural rulership, losing a lot of its power and being *held captive* by another sign's energy – for instance, a Mercury placed in Pisces is hardly intellectual, but instead perhaps you can find a very intuitive mind.

A planet *exalted* is a planet with a growing power; it is in a privileged placement, but not so much as if it were in a rulership. An exalted planet is in a sign where its energy has a good way to express itself. The opposite placement of planetary exaltation is the *fall*, in which the planet does not have full expression.

In short, when you study your birth chart, you will analyze the strength of the planets. Many ruling planets constitute an oasis and points from which you build a strong personality and get to live with a safe purpose. If you have many exalted planets, then you have great potential regarding those specific energies. Probably if you have many planets in detriment you put your abilities more to the service of others than to your own service. Finally, if you have many planets in fall, probably you will have very difficult times and experiences regarding that specific planetary energy.

SUN – The Sun symbolizes where you become aware of yourself and where you gain consciousness. It shows the particular way in which you shine. It can represent your father or your husband (the ideal image you hold of a husband). Rules Leo; is in detriment in Aquarius. Exalted in Aries; fall in Libra. It takes the Earth one year approximately to orbit the Sun.

MOON – The Moon represents your past emotions and memories, the way you instinctively react to things and people around you. It can represent your mother or wife (the ideal image you hold of a wife). Planetary rulership: Cancer; detriment: Capricorn. Exaltation: Taurus; fall: Scorpio. Its orbit is 28-30 days.

MERCURY – Mercury tells you how your intellect is. It depicts how you deal with commerce and business, industry and short travelling. Are you a good speaker and writer? How do you learn? How do you study? Rules Gemini and Virgo; is in detriment in Sagittarius and Pisces; exalted in Virgo and Aquarius, falls in Pisces and Leo. Orbit: approximately 88 days.

VENUS – Venus is about what you value and the way you love. It is related to love, beauty, universal harmony, elegance, fashion, cosmetics, and music. It can represent your feminine partner if you are a man. Rules Taurus and Libra; is in detriment in Scorpio and Aries. Exalted in Pisces, falls in Virgo. Its orbit is approximately 2/3s of a year.

MARS – Mars is the planet of action. How do you do things? Astrologically Mars represents power of will and energy. It governs armies and athletes. It can represent your masculine partner if you are a woman. Planetary rulership: Aries and Scorpio; detriment: Libra and Taurus. Exaltation in Capricorn; fall in Cancer. Orbit: approximately 2 years around our sun.

JUPITER – Sometimes you wonder: where is your luck? Jupiter can enlighten you. Your luck can come from law and wisdom, powerful people around you, your friends. It also represents your life philosophy and the way you deal with the system. It tells if you can become a good teacher, for instance, or an excellent lawyer or judge. Jupiter rules Sagittarius and co-rules Pisces. Jupiter is in detriment in Gemini and Virgo and is exalted in Cancer and falls in Capricorn. It orbits the Sun during 12 years.

SATURN – What are you afraid of? Saturn, also known as a «bad luck», somber planet, is simply the element that brings back what you have been doing; so it is a very important planet for karma analysis. It is inflexible and negative, meaning all things old, obstacles and resentment, but also important past lessons. Planetary rulership: Capricorn and co-rulership: Aquarius. Detriment is in Cancer and Leo. Exaltation is in Libra. Fall in Aries. It takes approximately 29 years to orbit the Sun.

URANUS – In what areas of your life do you need independence from others? How do you live? This is the revolutionary planet of the internet and all things electronic, but also of unpredictable events and major calamities. Rules Aquarius, is in detriment in Leo; exaltation in Scorpio and fall in Taurus. Orbit: 84 years around the Sun.

NEPTUNE – How do you live your spirituality? What is your personal view on transcendence? This planet governs all things spiritual and mystic; it is related with imagination and addiction and some spiritual and material dishonesty. It relates to how you serve the greater good. Planetary rulership: Pisces; detriment: Virgo. Exaltation: Leo; fall: Aquarius. It takes about 164 years to orbit our Sun.

PLUTO – How do you recover from major issues? Where do you have your energetic reserves? Pluto is the rebellious pull that drives us away from all things conventional; it is the genial field of those who analyze others in order to regenerate them and the society as a whole. It represents lust and all things secret and the absolute destruction of something or someone through manipulation and secret pacts. Rules Scorpio and is in detriment in Taurus. It is in exaltation in Aries and in fall in Libra. Orbit: 284 years.

Signs

What about the signs? What do they represent? In a short way, they are the essential quality of your energy as far as Astrology is concerned.

ARIES – The Warrior, entrepreneurial type. Athlete, business-oriented. It represents the pure joy of being here.

You may be determined, impulsive, ambitious, fiery, bold, energetic, independent, and bright. You may also be stubborn, impatient, with a strong urge for power, aggressive, sarcastic, arrogant, complaining, and ruthless.

TAURUS – The Farmer, worker type. It represents the joy of manifesting.

You may be simple, natural, extremely honest and friendly, dedicated, melodious, charming, persistent and artistic. You may also be very stubborn, greedy, a bit fanatic, envious, negligent and sloppy.

GEMINI – The talkative, the Writer. It represents the joy of communicating the message.

You may be versatile, smart, adaptable, ever-changing, graceful, and reasonable - an excellent communicator. However, you may also be superficial, dishonest, a quitter, gossiper and rarely generous.

CANCER – The Cook, Decorator type. It represents the joy of love.

Sentimental in the best sense, you may be strongly connected to your family and parents. Probably you are friendly, tolerant, modest, dedicated to your home, clean, methodical, and romantic. But you may also be vain, unstable, insecure, complaining, hypersensitive, negative and shy.

LEO – The Performer, Creative, King type. It represents the joy of self-expressing oneself.

You are bold, have an open mind and say what you must. You are friendly, optimistic, confident and a perfect leader. But, of course, you may also be a dictator, arrogant, cruel and vain, pompous and susceptible. It may happen you cannot stand to be overwhelmed or surpassed by someone else due to your vanity.

VIRGO – The Employee, Secretary or Pharmaceutical Type. It represents the joy of seeking perfection in all things.

This is the intellect sign par excellence, so probably you are trustworthy, methodical, conscious, hard-working and capable of surmounting a lot of obstacles. Probably you love studying and to be of service. Usually you may become a good writer, scientist and speaker. However, you must be very careful not to become a dandy, skeptic to the extreme, hypercritic or hypocrite. You can be boring, small-minded and sarcastic. Beware of greed and solitude.

LIBRA – The Diplomat. It represents the joy of maintaining a balance.

You may have a notorious balance, a harmonious nature, well proportioned, good-looking and harmonious, lover of art and beauty, well-raised, joyful, modest, patient, idealist, an excellent diplomat. But you may also be a playboy or playgirl, not concluding anything related to work or study; vain, extravagant, with a superficial charm, presumptive, frivolous and self-indulgent.

SCORPIO – The Witch or Psychotherapist. It represents the joy of transformation.

Determined, tenacious, bold, decided and aggressive, you may be very magnetic and have a very strong will. You are safe, honest, logic-thinking and observer, but also reserved and cautious. However, you can easily find yourself to be martial, aggressive, not understanding at all, oppressive, cruel, fanatic, suspicious, jealous and small-minded.

SAGITTARIUS – The Philosophical, Wandering type. It represents the joy of learning.

You may be extroverted, an assumed lover of life and nature, confident, open, optimistic, impulsive, positive, wise about other people, traveler, joyful and fun, productive. However, you may also be dishonest, arrogant, spender and easily fooled. You talk too much about what you do not know.

CAPRICORN – The hard-working, ambitious CEO type. It represents of joy of leaving something behind in order to be remembered.

You may be hard-working, extremely ambitious towards power and authority and specialist on patient effort. You are exact, meticulous, traditional, conservative, extremely cautious, solid, and an excellent work planner. But you may also be deeply depressive, worrying too much about the appearances, small-minded, hypochondriac, greedy, bitter, envious, inflexible and generally unhappy.

AQUARIUS – The Politician, Revolutionary type. It represents the joy of belonging being separated of the whole.

You may appear to the world as tolerant, friendly, fast in thought as in action, ingenious and creative; you may be an intellectual, independent, enthusiastic and a traveler. But you may also be very chaotic, eccentric, suspicious, psychosomatic, control freak, addict, weak and wandering through life with no purpose or goals.

PISCES – The Priest, Nurse type. It represents the joy of dissolution through universal love.

You may be friendly, peace lover and abnegated. Idealist, you probably have a good heart and receptive to others' pain, generous. However, you may also be undecided, guilty-addict, moody, susceptible, reserved, hypocrite, addict, masochist, a believer, hysterical.

Houses

The Houses of Zodiac state the «color» of your essential energy, that is to say where do you apply it:

FIRST HOUSE - Individual affirmation, physical aspect.

This House represents yourself: your temperament, personality and individual sense of Self. This House is concerned your physical appearance and the way you walk, talk, think and manifest yourself. It is your House of Character.

SECOND HOUSE – Values and what you own.

This is the House of your MONEY. Its study will provide you an idea about your financial matters at any given time as well as what you own and value. Do you have the ability to deal with what you value and own? This House shows your sources of income, benefits and costs – except for inheritances.

THIRTH HOUSE – Communication, siblings and studies.

This House relates to three different aspects of your life: family, short travelling and communication. Your relations with your siblings, aunts and cousins will be referred to here. This is the House of intellect and of speaking, writing and intimate relations. This also gives you a glimpse of travelling, especially as related to your work and education.

FOURTH HOUSE – Family, home, childhood, parents.

This House is about your ancestors, the way they affected your life and the influence of your parents in the way you live. This House portraits if you will get a stable home and a comfortable way of living or if, on the contrary, you will be torn apart by a divorce or have several house changes. If well read, this House can give you some insights about the later half of your life, usually the most important and a idea of the circumstances surrounding the end of your earthly life.

FIFTH HOUSE – Affirmation through self-worth or creativity.

This is the House of love, luck and life. Your impulses are described here: are you cold, normal or intense? This House can show you how many children you will have. This includes sports, your hobbies, artistic pursuits and all the fun – including gambling, games and speculation. Your popularity can be seen here.

SIXTH HOUSE – Health and job.

This House, in terms of Health, will show the illnesses afflicting you – as well as any surgical intervention. It shows how fragile or strong is your health and constitution. Will you be thin or fat? What is your favorite sort of food? All of this can be found out here.

About your job, this House describes accurately the type of relations you will establish with people subordinate to you in case you inherited a power or authority place. If you are an employee, this House can say a lot about your future perspectives.

SEVENTH HOUSE – Relationships, marriage and contracts.

This House relates with marriage and all kinds of contracts such as marriage and business. From this you can find out if you and your partner will live in harmony; if you will abandon home, if you will have a divorce or die too soon; if your partner will be tender toward you or not. All of this is portrayed in this House. You can find here as well the way in which the world in general will react to you: if you will be socially successful, if you will be onto business or onto politics. From this House you may learn some dangers lying within such relationships and some advantages you can seize in any occasion.

EIGHTH HOUSE – Sexuality, occultism and death.

This is the House of Death, because it tells approximately how you will die, though not the exact moment of your passing. You can be subjected to explosions, drowning or you can pass away from old age in your own bed; all of these chances are shown here. This House also portrays all inheritances you may get and warns about dangers and benefits you can get from money or other material assets. This House also gives an idea of your psychic possibilities.

NINTH HOUSE – Travelling.

This is the House of superior thought: religion, philosophy and all things related as beliefs and values systems. Here you can find out if you shelter hypocrite values. Long journeys, especially abroad, are all here: their goal, influence and success. In this House you can find out if you will live where you were born or if you will go abroad and stay there.

TENTH HOUSE – Career and social status.

This is the House of Career. This House tells you the specific talent you can use to build a career. Here you can find out your real talents. Sense of duty or the lack of it is also shown here, as well as probable power, status and fame.

ELEVENTH HOUSE – Associations, groups and friends.

In this House you can find out who your friends are and what sort of people will benefit your efforts, as well as those who only get in your way. Your hopes, political ideals, wishes, ambitions and possible accomplishments are also shown. This is very useful information.

TWELFTH HOUSE – Spirituality and intuition.

It is good to know your enemies and to be aware of them. You can see them in this House. Will you have close relations with charity institutions, hospitals and prisons? Will you be an employer or an employee? All of this you may find here on the Twelfth House.

Aspects

What about the aspects? These are angular distances measured among planets and they are aligned through an imaginary line that unites them to the center of the planet Earth (thus we are using a geocentric perspective) and then to some other planet. If a planet is near another by 10 or 11°, there is a *conjunction*. If there is a 60° angle, here we have a *sextile*. If there is a right angle (90°) there we have a square. If the planet is placed in an angle of 120° we have a *trine* and if the angle is of 180° we have an *opposition*.

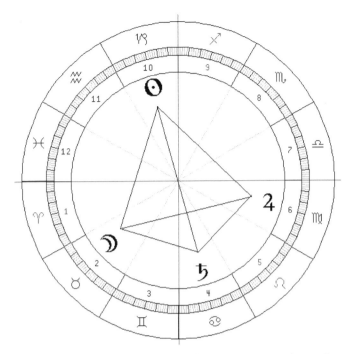

Conjunction between planets of different natures is unfavorable; if the planets have the same energetic nature the conjunction can be highly favorable. Planets of the same harmonious nature include the Sun, the Moon, Mercury, Venus, Jupiter, Uranus, Neptune. The most complex (but also most powerful) planets include: Mars, Saturn and Pluto. So any sort of aspect between those two planetary groups (for example, Venus and Mars) is potentially difficult.

Sextile is an aspect of good harmony and shows something we have to work out throughout this lifetime.

Square is synonym of a strong disharmony and shows where the internal conflict lies.

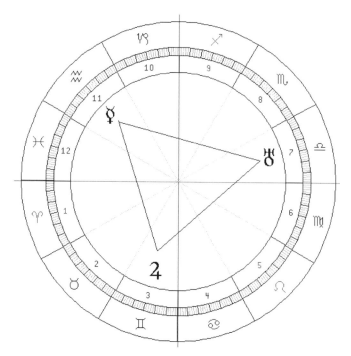

The trine shows a very good harmony between the planets and it is commonly accepted as a *gift* from previous lives.

Finally, the opposition refers to a strong external conflict regarding the planets involved.

There are many other aspects, minor and composed, that may be object of study on a birth chart. These are the most important ones.

Chapter 4

This chapter offers some experiments you can try out to know more about yourself, your family and friends. You may try it either with a traditional hand-made chart or with a computer-made chart. So try it!

Experiment 1: cast your own chart

It's very easy to do so. Nowadays there are many websites where you can cast your own chart. Try some in the *further reading* section. Get your parents' permission and/or help in doing this; you might need to know the time you were born, etc.

Experiment 2: count your Fire, Earth, Air and Water signs.

Take your chart and look for a table where your natal planets are distributed by elements and qualities. Count the ones placed in specific elements. This should give you a first image of your personality traits.

If you have many planets placed in Fire signs, you may consider yourself as a Fire person, rather impulsive, creative, intuitive, passionate and sometimes not very much persistent.

Is the majority of your planets is placed in Earth signs, probably you are determined, practical, hard-working, believe in what you can see and measure, and perhaps you have a difficult time talking about your emotions and weaknesses.

With many planets placed in Air signs, you may find yourself talkative, busy as a bee, intellectually driven, a good planner, but somehow a little dispersed.

Many Water planets may bring you a loving, beautiful, spiritual and family-driven personality, although you may find very difficult to keep private and academic/professional lives apart.

So there you go. There are 10 planets and 4 Elements. 2 or 3 planets in each sign refer to a very balanced personality, but usually there is one (or two) prevailing Element(s). So look out for yours!

Experiment 3: count your Cardinal, Fixed and Mutable signs

Take your chart and look for a table where your natal planets are distributed by elements and qualities. Count the ones placed in specific qualities. This should give you an idea of how you spend your energy.

If you have many planets placed in Cardinal signs, probably you are impetuous, success-driven, leader, fierce and explosive in the way you pursue your goals and use your energy.

Many planets in Fixed signs means stubbornness, which reflects on persistence, deliberation, anticipation and worrying about past things. So in terms of energy you tend to get clingy and too much attached to people and things. Grow out of it!

Finally, if your planets are concentrated in Mutable signs, change is what you value most. Routine and dullness are not for you, so you may vary everyday and not be able to get some stability in the way you use your energy. You may find yourself wanting a place to rest and to be left alone, but then new adventures will find their way to you.

There are 10 planets and 3 Qualities. 2 or 3 planets in each signs refer to a balanced personality, but usually there is one (or two) prevailing Qualitie(s).

Experiment 4: Find out your chart format: towards yourself, towards others, energy directed towards the outer world or the inner world

It is now time to check out your basic personality traits.

Your birth chart is divided by an horizontal axis from the Ascendant to the Descendent, which is the *space axis*. Then there is a vertical axis from the Medium Coeli to the Imum Coeli, which is the *time axis*.

There are 4 cardinal signs and houses in your astral chart. The first is the Ascendant (ASC), corresponding to the first house and to Aries sign. If you have most of your planets placed near the ASC area, your personality traits will be more directed to your own convictions and ideas than others'. In contrast, many planets near the Descendant (DSC) mean that you are much more susceptible to others' opinions and ideas and that being with others is essential for your happiness. You live towards others. This is the horizontal axis of analysis in your astral chart.

Of course we also can analyze the vertical axis, that comes up from the Imum Coeli (IC or FC) translating your inner world and heritages from the past until the Medium Coeli (MC) which refers to the outer success in the outside world and a career-oriented type of personality. So now you know.

Of course there are composites of these four personality types, for instance, you may have your planets near the IC and ASC meaning that for you the ideas stemming from your inner world are more important than influences from the outer world (this may happen if you become a writer, an actor, a psychologist, a therapist or if you have inherited good genes for practicing sports). And if you have many planets near the MC and DSC it may happen you become a successful diplomat, politician, public relations or business entrepreneur, once your success (MC) comes from strategic alliances with others (DSC). IC/DSC may mean you are a successful cooker, a fabulous student or even a wonderful interior decorator, architect or fashion designer. Finally, MC/ASC is usually found in leaders, CEO's, exceptional athletes or soccer/football players known worldwide. Remember: MC brings *projection* to what you do (Ivy League quality projection, for instance), whereas IC/FC brings you deep and mysterious heritages (such as gifts or rare talents). ASC means you base your actions and energy traits on *how you feel* and DSC just *depends on others* for doing something, be it a study session or a movie.

Check out your personality traits and learn to see what is your drive and what lies behind appearances.

Experiment 5: check out if you are a Sun or Moon tree

The Sun and the Moon are known as celestial bodies that give us light. They are the most personal planets in Western Tropical Astrology, so it is important to figure out if you are a Sun or

Moon tree. Why? That discovery process can provide some helpful insights to you.

So this experiment is very important and perhaps you can make some sense out of some things that happen to you since forever.

In general terms, the method I developed is based on the horizontal/vertical axis of astrological analysis. Here we consider that if you have many planets concentrated near the ASC you are under the Sun influence and the same happens when your planets are near the MC. The Moon will then be Lady of the DSC and the IC/FC.

What happens if you have a balance between both, meaning ASC/IC and DSC/MC traits? In this case, look at your solar sign. If it is an earth or water sign, chances are you are more lunar than solar. If it is a fire or air sign, then probably you are more solar than lunar.

Typically, unless some other things intervene, solar types are well-known, somehow popular, success-driven, usually with intense social lives, with classical beauty traits, but they also can become superfluous, vain and cruel to those less favored. Or they can become successful artists, sports or medical stars, because the Sun also has to do with physical activity, art in general and medicine. Lunar types are less favored when it comes to popularity and fashion, with less busy social lives, but huge talent, amazing beauty and deep thoughts arise between them. Usually their friendships are intense and their feelings passionate, but they always feel as if they do not fit in the surrounding environment.

So, find out what is your most important «light» planet! Are you a sunlight or a moonlight blessing?

Experiment 6: Find out the most important planetary energy in your birth chart

Well, all of this having being said, you find yourself a bit confused about what is really important in your birth chart. Between elements, qualities, chart formats and sun/moon polarities, which is the energy that most defines you? Probably you have felt several times that your solar sign in the horoscopes published does not quite fit with your characteristics... perhaps you find somehow attracted to other sign or other signs and find yourself thinking they have much in common with your core. What is happening?

As I said before, the Zodiac signs only describe your solar sign. Many times the Sun is not even close to being the most important planet in your birth chart, especially if you are a lunar type.

So, what can you do to find out what is your most important planetary energy? This planet will describe more than 50% of your personality traits, so once you find it be attentive about signs governed by that specific planet.

As you learned before, you are either a solar or lunar type. If you are a solar type, go and find where the Sun is in your chart. Find the planet nearer. That is the most important planet in your chart. If you are the lunar type, find the planet nearer the Moon and that will be the most important planet for you. If both of them are isolated, then look at the place where the planets concentrate the most. If they are near the ASC, find the one nearer. If they are near the MC, find the one nearer. And so forth regarding the DSC and the IC/FC. This is a simple way to find out what is the most important planet in your chart. You may be a Gemini in your solar sign, but if you are a lunar type and near the Moon you have Pluto, probably you will identify much more with Scorpio than with Gemini.

There are many ways to determine the most important planetary energies in your astral chart, but reducing all of them to the Sun sign and ASC is not a good idea. Please study this simple method and find out what it can do for you. Suddenly, it all starts to make a lot more sense...

Experiment 7: Analyze relationships between Elements and Qualities

A basic portrait of your personality characteristics can be found by crossing your Elements and Qualities placement. After counting your planets, cross the information about Elements and Qualities. Let's say, for instance, you have a lot of planets placed in Cardinal – Water. As we have seen before, Cardinal signs are used to put things in motion and water element refers to emotions. This may mean, for instance, that when you make a mistake you are the first (Cardinal) to apologize (Water); you may also be the first to try reconciling two of your best friends that no longer talk to each other.

This is one of some possible examples. Explore your own.

Experiment 8: Analyze relationships between Planets, signs and houses

This is a deeper level of analysis. Which planet is placed in which sign and in which house?

Let's take one example. Imagine that your most important planet is the Sun, placed in Taurus and in the Fourth House. As we have stated before, the Sun tells us where you shine and in what way you become conscious. So, your consciousness (the Sun) lies in the Farmer-type, working to manifest what you need and want (Taurus) and you need to do that through your family and home. Typically, this Sun in the Fourth House shows us someone that shines through something made at home (a writer, a private tutor) and also someone who can work (Taurus) to manifest things near home. Be also attentive regarding planets, signs and houses: your talent probably is inherited from one of your parents (Fourth House) and the manifestation of what you want will be probably slower-paced (Taurus and Fourth House) than fast.

There are hundreds of combinations possible, but if you follow simple reasoning about the nature, quality and manifestation of your unique energy, probably you will sort your chart and your family and friends' chart quite well.

Experiment 9: analyze some aspects of your birth chart

We approached before some major aspects of astrological analysis regarding the points uniting the planets. So let's start to explore them.

Imagine your most important planet is Saturn. Then you have to see what aspects it has regarding other planets. Personally I always follow the tables that come with the astral chart, I mean, the tables of interpretation that allow you to see what aspect one planet has relatively to others, starting with the Sun, the Moon, Mercury, Venus, Mars, Jupiter, Uranus, Neptune and Pluto. Let's say, for instance, Saturn presents a square to the Moon. As we said before, the square symbolizes a strong inner conflict, so we could dare to say that you had some conflicts regarding your mother (the Moon has to do with the maternal figure) and perhaps that you had some inner conflicts or sad memories of your childhood. Lack (Saturn) of affection (Moon), fear (Saturn), poor home conditions, old parents, something has provoked this tension in you. So let's explore the meanings of the planets and the basic guidance their aspects confirm or oppose.

You can explore all of this in your chart to any aspects. Please bear in mind that not all planets are compatible and that some conflicts are solved through your lifetime and transformed in a great asset as the time goes by. Astrology really allows you to transform yourself!

Conclusion

So you have learned the basics of Astrology analysis throughout this book. After trying it yourself, perhaps you decide (later) to take a course or to study further Astrology. Please be sure to choose the best teachers to learn from. And if you have any doubts please feel free to contact me.

However, be fully conscious that in order to learn about Astrology you have to study hard and to question yourself – no one can do that for you. Do not follow blindly all things taught to you. Discover some new data for yourself and develop new ways of perceiving the knowledge you have been given. That is a wonderful way to relate to Astrology.

In freedom,

Cynthia

Further reading

Cardoso, P. (2007-2009) – *Apontamentos e CD's do Curso de Astrologia [notes and CD's of Astrology course]*. Lisboa: copyright Paulo Cardoso.

Chermet-Carroy, S. (1999) – *A Astrologia e a Saúde [Astrology and Health]*. Lisboa: Editorial Estampa.

Crowmarsh, P. (1994) – *Astrologia: Os Segredos do Carácter Revelados pelas Estrelas [Astrology: the secrets of character revealed by the stars]*. 2.ª ed. Lisboa: Editorial Estampa.

Gulfoss, P. H. (2008) – *The Complete Book of Spiritual Astrology*. Woodbury, MN: Llewellyn Publications.

Hall, J. (2007) – *A Bíblia da Astrologia: Guia Completo do Zodíaco [The Astrology Bible: a thorough guide of the Zodiac]*. Lisboa: Dinalivro.

Lake, G. (2001) – *Símbolos da Alma: Descubra o seu Karma através da Astrologia [Soul symbols: find out your karma through astrology]*. Lisboa: Estampa, 2001.

Levine, R., Jawer, J. (2009) – *Your Astrology Guide 2010*. New York: Sterling.

Moita, M. (2009) - «Terra no Mapa Astral» [The Earth in your natal chart] in Boa Estrela, ano XV, 209, N.º 186, Outubro de 2009 pp. 19-24.

Martins, J. (1995) – *Zodiac: Astrologia por Computador [Zodiac: astrology on your computer]*. Lisboa: FCA.

Montéra, T. (2000) – *Tratado Prático de Astrologia Médica [a practical treaty of medical astrology]*. Mem Martins: Edições Europa-América.

Vega, P. (2002) – *Celtic Astrology: how the Mystical Power of the Druid Tree Signs can transform your Life*. Franklin Lakes, NJ: New Page Books.

Websites:

www.astro.com

www.cafeastrology.com

www.eastrolog.com

http://www.nova-lis.com/index.php

http://www.jadesolluna.com/

Charts from http://www.aquamoonlight.co.uk

Lunar calendar from
http://lunarscience.nasa.gov/articles/oldest-lunar-calendars

About the author

Cynthia Cassandra, aka Windsidh, goes by the name of Sara Timóteo. She is a Portuguese pagan and poetry writer. Cynthia works as a volunteer in Pagan Federation International through PFI – Associação Cultural Pagã in Portugal, thus contributing to a correct image of Paganism worldwide. A witch and oracular who always values freedom of being and thought as core values towards a real happiness, Cynthia is a professional astrologer and Tarot/oracle reader, a practitioner of the Iberic Tradition and a true polytheist devoted to the Radiant Gods and Goddesses of old.

Contact me:

windsidh@gmail.com

http://www.facebook.com/profile.php?id=1516661102

http://twitter.com/#!/CynthiaCassand

http://astrologyforth.blogspot.com/

About the publisher

Spero Publishing was founded in 2010. We believe that there should be an easier way to get quality writing published. Pagan owned and operated, we enjoy publishing products that may be overlooked by larger companies or mainstream media.

Among an increasing number of other products, we currently are excited to be offering our "A Child's Eye View" series, where we offer easy to understand books on a variety of religions and other spiritual topics.

We are also enthusiastic about our new devotional series in which we help our readers better connect to Deities from around the world.

Find us online at https://sites.google.com/site/speropublishing/ and on facebook at http://www.facebook.com/pages/Spero-Publishing/251479144907643

Also available through Spero:

You can find all of our products and services at:
https://sites.google.com/site/speropublishing/

A Child's Eye View:

The Child's Eye View series is designed to be short introductions to religions and spiritual practices. Written for people between 8 and 12 years old, they are easy to understand and fun for adults as well as teens and older kids. These are perfect short introductions not only for anyone interested in understanding paths other than their own, but also for parents, teachers, friends and others involved with the lives of children who practice these religions and paths.

Learn the facts about this little understood collection of religions by one of their most prolific authors, in a format easily digested by parents and young readers alike.

A Child's Eye View of Vodou,
by Dalton Miller

Vodou is alive and well in the United States and the Caribbean. Completely unlike Hollywood's image of it, it is a religion of love and joy that was created when African slaves were forcibly converted to French Catholicism. This book scratches the surface of this rich tradition.

A Child's Eye View of Wicca,
by Alan Leddon

An excellent "Wicca 101" course for children of Wiccan parents and for those adults who will work with them (like teachers and babysitters), this work touches on every aspect of Wiccan belief and practice.

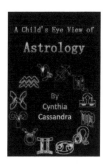

A Child's Eye View of Astrology,
by Cynthia Cassandra

Learn the meanings of 10 celestial bodies, the twelve houses, and the twelve Zodiac signs of western astrology, and how the interrelate. Learn to cast and interpret your own Astrological chart in this book by a professional Astrologer.

A Child's Eye View of Magick,
By Alan and Bekki Leddon

Written by a pair of parents who have a combined 45 years of Magickal practice, this is an ideal Magick 101 course for the serious Occultist as well as for beginning Pagans and Heathens of all ages. The previously secret teachings related to the Lesser Ritual of the Pentagram are revealed in one appendix, and another contains a list of historical divination practices.

A Child's Eye View of Tarot,
by Cynthia Cassandra

A simple, easy to follow do-it-yourself guide to the mysterious Tarot. This book is useful to people of all ages seeking to use the Tarot, or just to understand it. Fully illustrated, it is the ideal book for beginners, classrooms, and for seasoned readers wanting to brush up a bit.

A Spero Devotional Series:

Spero Publishing is excited to announce a new series of short devotionals dedicated to Deities from around the world. Each devotional offers its readers the opportunity to connect with the Deity in deeper and more profound ways through information, guided meditation, prayers and invocations. Collect them all or just keep an eye out for the Deities of your choice.

Poseidon: A Spero Devotional,
by Alan and Bekki Leddon

Learn about Poseidon and see what the Greek God with earth-shaking power who governs all bodies of water has to offer in your life.

Airmid: A Spero Devotional,
by Alan and Bekki Leddon

This insightful devotional helps its readers connect to the Celtic healing and warrior Goddess, Airmid. See what insight She can offer into your own life.

Thor: A Spero Devotional,
by Alan and Bekki Leddon

This work introduces the mighty Norse God of Storms! Learn a bit of His history, and enjoy the included recipe for non-alcoholic mead!

Pele: A Spero Devotional,
by Alan and Bekki Leddon

Connect with and better understand this Hawaiian Volcano Goddess. Learn how to work with this passionate Goddess to add new spark to your life!

Thoth: A Spero Devotional,
by Alan and Bekki Leddon

Thoth was the Greek name for the Egyptian God Tahuti, the God of Writing, Cosmic Balance, Magic, and Science. This devotional will help you connect with and better understand both Tahuti and the mysteries of the universe.

Free as a PDF to our facebook fans, this is otherwise available for purchase.

Lakshmi: A Spero Devotional,
by Alan and Bekki Leddon

A free gift from Spero Publishing, this devotional is designed to help you connect with the loving Hindu Goddess of abundance. Use this information to welcome Her into your life!

Other books include:

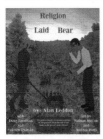

Religion Laid Bear, by Alan Leddon

This is an essential guide to Arctolatry (Bear worship) and the first book ever written on the subject.

The Bear may be mankind's first god. Bear's activities connected him at once with the sun, with vegetation, and with the underworld. Reconnect with our ancient deity through 38 shamanic practices and a simple but potent ritual of worship, designed to appeal to both Pagans and Heathens. Learn step by step to make ritual tools, and see how 40 popular mythological figures show the import of the Bear to our long ago ancestors. The book is jam packed with biological data on extent and extinct bear species, and even discusses the hows and whys of Shamanism from the perspective of modern science.

The author pledges to donate a portion of the proceeds of this work to organizations that work to preserve bears in the wild and to end tragic activities such as the milking of bile from captive bears.

Honoring Sigyn:
the Norse Goddess of Constancy,
by Galina Krosskova

Sigyn is the epitome of the good wife and mother. She is loving, loyal, caring, kind hearted, attentive to the needs of Her husband and children. Don't underestimate Her though - She is a Norse Goddess!

Written by a lifelong Sigyn's Woman, this devotional traces all of Sigyn's known appearances in the Lore and adds to this the lifetime experiences and UPGs of two ardent followers of the Goddess.

The Cavern's Wise Woman: The Bear Goddess, by Annie Welch

This book describes Arctolatry, Bear worship, and how to connect with this ancient, cross cultural religious path through understanding and working with Arta. Learn how you can personally connect with Her, use the tools of Her worship, understand Her holy tides, and experience the lessons She wants people to learn to have a more rewarding, more fulfilling life.

A Little Girl Growing, by Bill Jutz

Everyone grows up. For some, this is an easy experience. In this, the first of 5 books of tear-jerking poetry, Bill Jutz captures the experience of growing up different in a world of conformity. Explore the LGBT experience in its most heartfelt form.

Sydney and John by Sheila Parker

Witness how the power of friendship can overcome the fear of a bully in this book for slightly more advanced early readers.

We'd also like to recommend...

Andrea Potts works in a number of media. She is a surprisingly good vocalist, becoming popular in Madison coffee shops and outdoor venues. She also paints and draws, and has contributed artwork to books. To see a sampling of her paintings and to purchase CDs of her original music, please see her website: http://www.andreapotts.com/

Norse Inspired Creations

For the finest quality Norse leather and horn art, runic jewelry, and more... http://urnesashtree.webs.com/

Quality Pagan Inspirational Music

Check out Heartbeat at http://www.heartbeatband.com/ for a positive experience in inspirational Pagan music.

Printed in Great Britain
by Amazon.co.uk, Ltd.,
Marston Gate.